The Railway Children

A musical

Book and Lyrics by Julian Woolford
Music by Richard John

From the novel by E. Nesbit

Samuel French — London
www.samuelfrench-london.co.uk

THE RAILWAY CHILDREN

The Railway Children was first produced at Sevenoaks Playhouse, on 3rd December 2005, with the following cast:

Perks	Paul Henry
Father	Charles Shirvell
Mother	Susannah Fellows
Peter	Chris Crompton
Carol Singers	Maria Holley
	Neil Ditt
	Brendan Cull
Cook	Karen Clegg
Ruth	Claire Taylor
Roberta	Emily Bull
Phyllis	Lucy Brushett/
	Rachel Bartholomeusz
Mr Barrie	Brendan Cull
Dr Forrest	Neil Ditt
Lord Fleet	Charles Shirvell
Mrs Ransome	Claire Taylor
Gert	Maria Holley
Mrs Perks	Karen Clegg
Old Gentleman	Nicholas Smith
Rushing Man	Brendan Cull
Szczepansky	Charles Shirvell
Engine Driver	Neil Ditt
Jim	Brendan Cull
Londoners	Claire Taylor
	Maria Holley
	Karen Clegg
Vendor	Charles Shirvell
Customer	Neil Ditt

Children's Chorus
Megan Barker, Georgia Brown, Hollie Evans, Rebecca
Hairs, Rosie Jenner, Emma Sweet, Karl Warner, James
Webster, Charlotte Wilson, Jade Wood, Stephanie Barrett,
Oliver Christopher, Sophie Cook, Olivia Davy, Laura
Hayward, Leanne Kyte, Annabelle Lake, Glyn Pritchard,
Kiri Rayner, Paige Stapleton

Directed by Julian Woolford
Musical Supervisor: Richard John
Choreographed by Chris Hocking
Set designed by Charles Camm
Lighting designed by Emma Chapman
Sound designed by Dominic Bilkey
Costume supervisor: Rodney Worth
Musical Director: Laurence Mark Wythe
Vocal and dance arrangements: Richard John
Russian translation: Simon Hollands
Photography: Robert Workman

CHARACTERS

Perks, a stationmaster
Father, a civil servant
Mother, his wife
Peter, his son
Ruth, his maid
Cook, his cook
Bobbie (Roberta), his daughter
Phyllis, his younger daughter
Carol Singers
Mr Barrie
Dr Forrest
Lord Fleet
Ethel
Flo
Mrs Ransome
Gert
Mrs Perks
Old Gentleman
Colin Perks
Elsie Perks
Ginger Perks
Patch Perks
Rushing Man
Szczepansky
Engine Driver
Jim
Customer
Lady
Gossip
Housewife
Vendor

DOUBLING

In the original production the following doubling was used

Men
1 Perks
2 Old Gentleman
3 Father/ Lord Fleet/ Szczepansky/ Vendor
4 Carol Singer/ Dr Forrest/ Engine Driver/ Customer
5 Carol Singer/ Mr Barrie/ Rushing Man/ Jim

Women
1 Mother
2 Bobbie
3 Ruth/ Mrs Ransome/ Gossip
4 Cook/ Mrs Perks/ Lady
5 Carol Singer/ Gert/ Housewife

Children play all other roles, and in the original production the Paperchase Ballet was danced by Jim, Women 3,4,5 and additional children.

SCENES AND MUSICAL NUMBERS

ACT I

SCENE 1   The London House and Surrounding Streets
           No. 1: Prologue
           No. 2: Christmas is Here!
           No. 3: You Can Never Return

SCENE 2   Charing Cross Station
           No. 4: Together
           No. 5: Change of Scene

SCENE 3   The Cottage
           No. 6: Together (reprise)
           No. 7: The Great Green Dragon

SCENE 4   The Hillside

SCENE 5   The Station
           No. 8: All on Time

SCENE 6   Inside the Cottage
           No. 9: All on Time Play Off
           No. 10: You Might Make a Friend (1)
           No. 11: You Might Make a Friend (2)
           No. 12: The Old Gentleman's Letter
           No. 13: You Might Make a Friend (3)

SCENE 7   The Station Platform
           No. 14: Posh Talk
           No. 15: Posh Talk Playoff

SCENE 8   The Cottage Garden and Kitchen
           No. 16: Lullaby

SCENE 9   The Railway Carriage and The Hillside
           No. 17: The Railway Children

SCENE 10   The Cottage Garden
           No. 18: 'Til the Day

SCENE 11   The Hillside, Outside the Tunnel
           No. 19: Act One Finale

Time: Christmas 1905 to September 1906

The original cast recording is available on TER and JAY records.
A Vocal Selection and Vocal Score are available on sale from Samuel French Ltd. and orchestral parts are available on hire from Samuel French Ltd.

AUTHOR'S NOTE

E. Nesbit's story, unlike the work of her male contemporaries, is firmly set in the real world. Whilst J.M. Barrie was writing about fairies and flying boys, and Kenneth Grahame was writing about a mischievous Toad, *The Railway Children* is based on Nesbit's own memories of her Kent childhood. This musical sets out to create a theatrical language for her story. There are a few points to bear in mind, which I hope might clarify the way the story is told.

Although the script is broken down into scenes, each act should be played as one long continuous sequence, without any blackouts. Scenes dissolve into each other and sometimes the musical numbers take place inside the thoughts of the characters. You will also find that songs sometimes continue into subsequent scenes.

Bear in mind that the whole musical takes place in Mr Perks' memory. This is not always a reliable memory, and when in the Prologue he sings of how Roberta *told* him about the beginning of the story, that is precisely what he means. He cannot remember it himself, so our original London set was a sepia idea of London as imagined by Perks, based on photographs he might have seen. The country, on the other hand, is a place he remembers well — particularly the station, so was more detailed (and colourful) in its physical realization.

Perks is the only character that can address the audience. He must be great fun, and the audience generally adore him. Let him be physically funny, but there is a temptation to step out of character in this part and become an actor commenting on the piece, rather than Perks. Keep any ad libs completely correct to time and character. A great Perks will lead the show and be a delight whenever he is onstage, because his relationship with the audience is the same fun and kindly "uncle" that he is with the Railway Children.

The emotional core of the musical is Bobbie's rite of passage to adulthood over one long, adventurous summer. Her thoughts develop from childish simplicity in *Christmas is Here!* and *Posh Talk* to maturity in *Nothing to Fear* and *Nearly Autumn*. You need a young actress who can make the transition from girl to woman. It is worth remembering that Bobbie, Peter and Phyllis are real children, not china dolls: they should not be played too prim and proper.

This musical is quite a challenge — or a gift — to a designer and I would encourage as much imagination as you can muster. It is probably worth understanding how the trains were represented in the original production, although there are many solutions to these moments, so these are by no means definitive. The station was a piece of set that came on from the stage right wing. Passengers getting off the trains entered from in front of the set, accompanied by a generous dose of smoke and copious sound effects of trains and doors slamming. It was as if the trains were running along the first row of the auditorium. For the songs that happen in train carriages; *Together* was staged first carrying, then sitting on suitcases, and *The Railway Children* was simply staged with the Old Gentleman walking from upstage and exiting on the other side downstage.

The biggest technical challenge is the train at the end of Act I. Ours came out of a tunnel that had been concealed in the centre of the back wall up until the beginning of the scene (and became the same tunnel used in Act II). The train was a truck, quite tall, in the shape of the front of the train as if you are looking straight at it. It was not more than about a metre deep, and was accompanied by the music, generous helpings of smoke and roaring train sound effects played at furious volume. The piece of set wasn't that big, but we never failed to get a round of applause for its entrance.

If you want to, please feel free to localize the story, especially if you are performing it in the UK. Change Peter's line about Kent and use a local station name for the fun of it.

You may find there are one or two discrepencies between the Original Cast Album CD and the material published. Where there are, please always use the material published in this script and vocal score.

Finally, if you have any questions or want to contact us to tell us about your production, please email us at woolford.andjohn@virgin.net and we will endeavour to be as much help as we can.

Julian Woolford, London 2006

For Stephen,
With Love

JW

"A Railway isn't just carriages and a locomotive
and a permanent way. It's a sort of door."

Clifford Dyment, *The Railway Game*

ACT I
SCENE 1

The London House and Surrounding Street, Christmas 1905

In darkness, a train whistle is heard and the music begins

No. 1: Prologue

The Lights begin to build. A spotlight comes up on Perks. He has his back to the audience. He turns and sings

Perks

There's the sound of the whistle,
The train's coming in,
And you wait short of breath,
As a journey begins.
With each day that you live,
How your life will be changed,
Like the stations you find
On a trip on a train.

He comes a little nearer the audience

Now sit back and get comfy
So our story can start.
And I'll try to remember,
(But I'm not very smart).
There's a girl that I knew,
She might be just like you,
And she dreamed of adventures
As kids often do.

The Lights build and reveal the outside of a Victorian villa, in a prosperous London Street

Now all tales have beginnings,
This one starts far from here
She told me of how,
It's a place she held dear.

And she said it began,
Upon one Christmas time,
At a London address,
Known as house, twenty-nine.

The house opens to show a comfortable drawing-room interior with a Christmas tree, the family, and a children's Christmas party in full swing. The children are mainly playing on the floor with a new train set. Outside Carol singers and Urchins gather around the home

No. 2: Christmas is Here!

All (*singing*)   Christmas is here again!
Sing of good cheer again!
Sing of a manger and shepherds and silent night!
Christmas is here again!
Sing of good cheer again!
Sing carols and stars so light —
Burning bright!

Perks (*speaking*) And like many families, this one had a mother, and a father...

Father (*singing*)   This time of the year,
Best time of the year,
Wife, family, home, call this man lucky!
Mother   Best time of the year,
Our time of the year,
You free from your work, being so near ——
Peter   Look, look at the train!
Peter ⎫
Mother ⎬   Look, look at the train!
Mother ⎫
Father ⎬   And each year like the last ——

Adults   Christmas is here again!
Sing of good cheer again!
Children   Christmas
Christmas
All   Sing of a stocking and reindeer and Santa Claus!
Children   Santa Claus
All   Christmas is here again!
Sing of good cheer again!
Give presents to you and yours ——
All because ——

The carolling singers bring Mother to the door to invite them in for mince pies and a drink

Carol Singers	Christmas night, so very long ago,
	Jesus Christ, our saviour was born,
	To save our souls from all of our earthly sins,
	On a cross, crownéd with thorns.
	What a child, what a man born this night,
	In a manger, in a stall.
	We must not forget the children's love,
	For a child saved us all.

Perks (*speaking*) And servants!

Cook ⎱ **Ruth** ⎰	Christmas is here again,
Cook	Food getting dear again!
Cook ⎱ **Ruth** ⎰	Hundreds of thousands of callers all droppin' by!
Cook	All for a taste of my pies.
Ruth	Christmas is here again,
Cook	Mince pies and beer again,
	Can't wait 'til Boxing Day then I can quietly die!

A Caller enters

Ruth (*to the Caller*)	Good-evening so glad you came!
All	Christmas is here again!
	Sing of good cheer again!
	Sing of a banquet of turkey and ham laid out!
	Christmas is here again!
	Sing of good cheer again!
Ruth ⎱ **Cook** ⎰	Sing carrots and brussel sprouts!
	And pigging out!

Perks (*speaking*) And that girl I told you about --

Bobbie (*singing*)	Why can't my life be like the books I read?
	Princes and kings, pirates and sea.
	Every new book brings me another tale,
	All I'm left with is a dream.
	Thrilling stories!
	Bold adventures!
	When will mine begin?

	This time next year,
	One year older,
	What might happen then?
Peter	Look, look at the train!
Peter	
Mother	Look at the train.
Father	
Bobbie	
Mother	And each year like the last.
Father	
Bobbie	This time next year,
	One year older,
	Why can't my life be like the books I read?
	Thrilling stories,
	Bold adventures,
	When will my life begin?
Mother	This time of the year,
Father	Best time of the year,
	Wife, family, home
	Call this man lucky!
	Best time of the year,
	Our time of the year,
	You free from your work, being so near
Children	Christmas is here!
	Sing of good cheer.
	Sing of a stocking and reindeer and Santa Claus.
	Santa Claus.
	Christmas is here again!
	Sing of good cheer again!
	Give presents to you and yours.
Ruth	Christmas is here again!
Cook	
	Food getting dear again!
	Hundreds of thousands of callers all droppin' by!
	All for a taste of my pies, again!
	Mince pies and beer again,
	Sing carrots and brussel sprouts.
Carol singers	Christmas night, so very long ago,
	Jesus Christ, our saviour was born,
	What a child, what a man born this night,
	For a child saved us all.
Children	Christmas is here again!
Bobbie	Sing of good cheer again!
	Sing of a stocking and reindeer and Santa Claus

(*not Bobbie*)	Santa Claus!
Mother	Christmas is here!
Mother ⎫	Our time of year!
Father ⎭	
Father	Call this man lucky!

Female Carollers ⎫	Christmas is here!
Ruth ⎬	Sing of good cheer.
Cook ⎭	Stockings mean Santa Claus.

Carol Singers	Christmas is here!
	Sing of good cheer
	Sing of a stocking and reindeer and Santa Claus,
Mother ⎫	
Father ⎬	And each year like the last!
Bobbie ⎭	
Children	Christmas is here again!
	Sing of good cheer again!
Mother ⎫	
Father ⎬	Sing of good cheer!
Bobbie ⎭	
Carollers ⎫	Christmas is here!
Ruth ⎬	Sing of good cheer,
Cook ⎭	
All	Give presents to you and yours
Basses	All because ——
Tenors	All because ——
Altos & Basses	All because ——
Sopranos	All because ——
All	All because ——
	Christmas is here!!!!

*By the end of the number, the Carol Singers and Party Guests have left the
house*

The toy train, which has been running around the floor, suddenly explodes

Peter Daddy, what's happened?
Father I don't know.
Phyllis It's broken.
Peter Is it, Father?
Father But I don't think it can be too bad. I'll fix it.

There is a knock on the door

Mother Who'd be knocking now?
Peter When will you fix it?

Ruth enters

Ruth (*entering*) Excuse me, sir, there's two gentlemen to see you. I've shown them into the study.
Father I'll fix it when I come back. Thank you, Ruth.

Father exits

Mother Who is it, Ruth?
Ruth Ma'am, I think they want you to go in too.
Mother (*to all*) Now you all play nicely. I'll be back in a minute and then we'll have Christmas cake.
Phyllis Hooray. I love cake. Mummy, you're a darling!

Mother exits

Bobbie Who is it, Ruth?
Peter I want Daddy to come back and mend my engine. It's new.
Bobbie What's going on?
Ruth Ask me no questions and I'll tell you no lies.
Peter Can you find out how long they are going to be?

Ruth exits

Perks appears in his own space

No. 3: You Can Never Return

Perks (*singing*)   With a knock and a shudder,
A lurch, a start,
An adventure's beginning,
And it's time to depart.

Ruth enters

Ruth (*speaking*) Put away your presents, take down the decorations, this year Christmas is cancelled.

Ruth exits

Perks (*singing*)   And you know you'll be changed
By the things that you learn,
So you know, in a way,
You can never return.

Perks exits

SCENE 2

Charing Cross Station

Bobbie, Peter and Phyllis are revealed with some luggage. There is no sign of Mother or Father

Peter I don't understand why we have to move to the country. And Kent of all places.

Bobbie Silly! Because Father had to go away on business.

Peter But why does that mean we can't stay at home?

Bobbie I asked Ruth last night and she said we will know soon enough.

Peter You asked her! Mother told us not to!

Bobbie If you could go to bed without caring whether Mother was worried or not, I couldn't. So there!

Peter Well, I am going to find out what the problem is.

Mother enters, unseen by Peter

I don't care if Mother doesn't want us to know. I want to know and I am old enough. I don't care what Mother says. She's being silly, just like a grown up.

Mother Is she now? We'll see about that.

Peter (*sheepishly*) Sorry.

Mother Children, I know you want to know where Daddy is, and you will in good time. But until then, I want you to help me and not make things more difficult than they already are. Will you?

Bobbie ⎱
Phyllis ⎰ (*together*) Yes

Mother Peter?

Peter Yes, Mother.

Mother I don't want you to ask me any questions; or anyone else. Promise?

Bobbie Father's in a Government Office. Is it about the Government?

Mother No questions. Yes it is.

Peter But why do we have to go and live in the country?

Mother We are going to live in the country and that's all there is to it.

Phyllis Will Ruth be coming to join us?

Mother No.

Children Hooray!

Mother looks at the children, admonishing their lack of manners. They look worried, then she smiles

Mother Hooray!

No. 4: Together

Peter But I hate the country. There's no zoos or shops or underground trains. There's only cows and sheep. They're boring.

Mother Peter!

(*Singing*)   The country isn't boring,
                          Only dull, if you think that way.
                          There are wonders in store,
                          A world to explore,
                          Adventures every day.

Peter (*speaking*) But it's not like London. It's not exciting.

Mother (*speaking*) No, it's not like London

(*Singing*)   The country's not the city
                          We can leave the fog behind,
                          And London smoke and grime,
                          And grit and crime,
                          For adventure of a different kind.

Bobbie (*speaking*) Will Father come and visit us?

Mother No, I don't think so.

Bobbie Why not?

Mother No questions. You promised.

Peter How long will Father be away?

Mother No questions.

Phyllis Won't he even see us on our birthdays?

Mother No questions.

Bobbie What will we do without our Daddy?

Peter
Phyllis } (*together*) What will we do?

As the number is performed, they travel to the cottage, but there is no sense of them actually being in a train, rather that they are at the station when the number starts and at the cottage by the time it has finished. They use their suitcases as seats during the following verse which takes place in a railway carriage

Mother (*speaking*) So many questions. Children don't worry. We will still be together. Don't worry.

(*Singing*)   Together, there will still be sunlight,
                          Together, there will still be rain,
                          And picnics in summer
                          And days by the sea
                          And walks and trips on a train.

Peter (*speaking*) Like this one?

Mother Yes.
    (*Singing*)   Together, there will still be birthdays—
Phyllis I'm eight soon!
Mother   — And maybe a trip to a zoo —
Peter I like the zebras best.
Mother   And of course we'll be missing him,
                       Wishing that he were here too,
                       Together, we're sure to pull through.
                       Together, there will still be springtime,
                       In autumn, the leaves will fall,
                       With stories by firesides,
                       And crumpets for tea
                       And visits to large stately halls
    (*Speaking*) Listen!
    (*Singing*)   Together there will be no schooldays,
Children (*speaking*) Hooray!
Mother   But lessons taught by me to you,
                       And although we'll be missing him,
                       Wishing that he were here too,
                       Together, we're sure to pull through.
    (*Speaking*) Now it's your turn.

The song becomes a game, Mother points at whoever she wants to go next and they have to come up with a word. The children warm to her

All   Together,
Mother   There will still be ——
Bobbie   Music!
All   Together,
Mother   There will still be
Phyllis   Games!
Peter   And cowboys ——

Mother points at Peter again

                     — and dinosaurs,
Bobbie   And bicycle rides,
Phyllis   And dogs

Mother points at Phyllis again

                     And pantomime dames
All   Together,

Mother	There will still be
All	Christmas!
	With presents and Santa Claus too!
	And although we'll be missing him,
	Wishing that he were here too,
Phyllis	Together,
Peter	Together,
Roberta	Together
Mother	Together,
All	Together we're sure to pull through!

SCENE 3

The Cottage

The number ends and they are in a dimly-lit cottage with sparse furniture. There is silence and then the sound of scratching

Their buoyant mood leaves them quickly

Mother Oh no. I asked her to light a fire.
Phyllis What's that scratching noise?
Peter I expect it's just rats!

Phyllis screams

Bobbie Peter!
Mother Now, isn't this fun! You always said you wanted an adventure. I asked Mrs Viney to leave us some supper, so I suppose she will have left it on the table.

Mother lights a lamp and looks

It's not here. Oh no, she's just walked off with the money and not left the food.
Peter Then we won't have any supper at all.
Phyllis I wish Father was here, he'd know what to do.

Bobbie kicks her

Ow! Why are you kicking me, Bobbie?
Bobbie Me? Sorry, leg slipped.
Mother Children! I have an apple for each of you I kept from the journey. (*She gives them each an apple*) You can have that, and I'll get up early in the morning and go down to the village and buy some bacon and eggs for breakfast. How does that sound?

Phyllis Why can't a servant go?

Mother I told you darling, we don't have servants here.

Phyllis I'm not sure I like that.

Mother Nor am I, but lots of people live without servants. It won't take us long to get used to it.

Peter I'm cold and hungry and there's no servants. Why can't we go back home?

Bobbie Because we can't.

Mother Think of it as an adventure.

Phyllis I don't like this adventure.

Mother Now, go and decide which bedrooms you want. Get into bed and I'll be up in a minute to say good-night. Take your apples.

Peter Come on, first one upstairs gets first pick!

The Children rush off

Mother watches them go

No 6: Together (Reprise)

Quite business-like, Mother begins to unpack. She looks around the cottage and sees it as a dingy, cramped, unfriendly place. She unpacks a framed photograph of her husband

Mother (*singing*)   And although we'll be missing him,
                              Wishing that he were here too...

Mother sits and cries

The Lights fade on Mother

Perks appears in his own space

Perks (*singing*)   You may enter a tunnel,
                             And you get quite a fright —
                             All the lights are dimmed,
                             Like you're travelling at night.
                             As the darkness descends,
                             How your heart may feel tight,
                             Oh, be sure that at sometime,
                             You'll return to the light.

The music continues. The Lights cross-fade to the next morning in the cottage. The room is empty and filled with sunlight. There is food laid out on another table

Perks exits

Bobbie enters carrying a dress. She is followed by Phyllis wearing a night-dress. She is tired and rubbing sleep from her eyes

Phyllis Wassamarrar?
Bobbie Come on. Put this on.

Bobby hands Phyllis the dress, which she pulls over her night-dress

Don't you remember? We're in the new house! No servants or anything. Let's creep down to the village and get the things for breakfast. I've woken Peter. He's getting dressed.

Peter enters

Peter (*shouting*) I'm ready!
Bobbie Shhh!
Phyllis Shhh!
Peter Shhh! Look!

They turn to look and see food all laid out on the table

We must have missed it last night. (*He starts to eat the food*)
Bobbie It's a pretty house.
Phyllis It's darling.
Bobbie Listen!

There is the sound of the train in the distance

No. 7: The Great Green Dragon

Peter A railway! If we can hear it, it must be nearby. Let's go and see it!

Bobbie and Peter rush off

Phyllis stuffs food in her pockets and mouth and follows them

Phyllis Wait for me!

Phyllis exits

SCENE 4

The Hillside

The Children rush to the top of the hill and wave at the train below

There is the noise of the train rushing by

Bobbie It's like a great green dragon breathing fire.
Peter It's ginormous!
Bobbie Ginormous isn't a word! It's gigantic or enormous.
Phyllis It's big!
Bobbie The Great Green Dragon's going where Father is! It could take our love to Father.
Peter Dragons don't carry people's love.
Bobbie This one will.
Phyllis Let's all wave to the Dragon as it goes by.
Bobbie If it understands, it'll take our love to Father, and if it doesn't, three waves aren't much.

The music swells

The Children wave and shout

Bobbie Take our love to Father!
Children Take our love to Father!
Bobbie Look, can you see that Old Gentleman? There in the third carriage! He's waving back!
Peter Look, there's the station! Let's go and see it.

SCENE 5

The Station

The Children rush to the station

Bobbie Isn't it sweet.
Peter It's tiny! It's not like Euston or St Pancras. They're real stations.

Perks comes through the station door

Perks Hallo, there.
Peter Hallo, sir.

Perks Sir? That's a bit posh. You must be the new lot staying at Three
Chimneys Cottage.

Peter We are. We're the new pennants.

Bobbie Tenants.

Perks Bless you. Mrs Ransome told me all about you. From London, aren't
you? Well, you won't find it like London round here. It's clean. And what's
your names then?

Bobbie I'm Roberta, but everyone calls me Bobbie.

Peter I'm Peter. Mother says while Daddy's away, I'm the oldest man and
so I am head of the housework.

Perks Does she now.

Phyllis And I'm Phyllis.

Perks And I'm Mr Perks. Staying at the Three Chimneys long, or just here
for a visit?

Peter We're not sure.

Bobbie Mother says she should know more after her trip to London next
week.

Peter We're here until Father's finished some business.

Phyllis (*conspiratorially*) It's top secret.

Perks (*tapping his nose*) I see. Now then, like trains then, do you?

Peter Yes, sir.

Perks Well, you're welcome to pop down here anytime you like, then.

Peter Mr Perks, are you a enthoosiasm?

Perks Not half!

Peter Which is your favourite train?

Perks Why, it'd have to be the Great Green Dragon. Quite 'stronery.

Bobbie The Great Green Dragon? That's what we called it!

Perks Well, that's what it looks like, a Great Green Dragon. Breathing fire!
Rushing in and out of tunnels! Like a Great Green Dragon.

Phyllis Mr Perks, you're a darling.

No. 8: All on Time

Perks (*singing; colla voce*) If you pass through this door
There are wonders in store,
For this is the door to elation,
And once you've passed through
There are marvels to view
And a cause for a grand celebration.

*They open the station door and throughout the following move through the
station and on to the platform*

Come on in, look around,
And you will be spellbound
By the sounds and the smells that surround you,
By the deafening din
When the train's coming in,
When it's gone then the calm will astound you.
Will you look at the gleam
Of the ticket machine,
I've been cleaning since quarter to seven,
And there's blossoms in bloom
Near the old waiting room,
Why this station is my bit of heaven.
And the platforms through here,

They move on to the platform, but Phyllis lingers in the station building

Will you come along dear,
There is much that I'd so like to show you,
I'm a railway man,
And if you are a fan,
I am glad that I'm getting to know you.

All on time,
That's the way to run a railway.
All on time,
The pride of a job done well.
From Land's End to John o'Groat's,
Every trav'ler surely votes,
There's nothing so fine as a railway line,
Running all on time.

During the next verse other Villagers start to arrive at the station and are introduced

All the folks who pass through,
Often shout,

Perks ⎫
Villagers ⎬   "how d'you do",
Perks ⎭

I am friends with the whole population,
From ladies and lords,
To the populous hordes,
For the station's their link to the nation.
And I'll introduce you,
Without further ado,

Mr Barrie's our dear village grocer,
Dr Forrest has skill, makes you well when you're ill, and

Perks
Villagers }   Lord Fleet —
Perks   — You must greet with an ——
Perks
Villagers }   "Oh sir".
Perks

And there's Ethel and Flo,
(They're the twins, don't you know),
From the post office here's Mrs Ransome,
And that naughty girl, Gert,
Is a bit of a flirt,
Why she told Mrs Pugh that I'm handsome!
But the girl from the start,
Who fair captured my heart,
We were married in dear Aberystwyth.
And the light of my life,
Is my trouble and strife,
She's the girl that I once had a tryst with.

Villagers   All on time
Perks
Villagers }   That's the way to run a railway.
Villagers   All on time,
Perks   The pride of a job done well.
Villages }   From Land's End to John o'Groat's,
Every trav'ler surely votes,
There's nothing so fine as a railway line,
Running all on time.

Perks   There is nowt to compare
With the smell in the air
Of an engine departing the station,
Or of taking a ride
In the wide countryside,
For a right bloomin' mighty sensation.
From the town she departs,
Off to faraway parts,
Where nobody had previously trodden.
As she clatters along,
Her industrial song,
Is the essence of all that is modern.
In the engine you're drowned
By the deafening sound
Of the monster you have to keep feeding,
As you shovel the coal

In her fiery hole,
It's the fuel for her magic stampeding.
With her smuts and her coke
And her steam and her smoke,
How she thunders in charge of her wagons.
When the station's in view,
Then the brakes are pulled to,
With a hiss like an asthmatic dragon!

Villagers   All on time,

Perks ⎫
Villagers ⎬   That's the way to run a railway.

Villagers   All on time,

Perks ⎫   The pride of a job done well.
Villagers ⎬   From Land's End to John o'Groat's,
Every trav'ler surely votes,
There's nothing so fine as a railway line,
Running all on time.

*Dance break. Each of the villagers has a solo section during which they
indicate their jobs and characteristics*

All   All on time,
That's the way to run a railway.
All on time,
The pride of a job done well.
From Land's End to John O'Groats,
Every trav'ler surely votes,
There's nothing so fine as a railway line,

Sopranos   Running ——
Basses   Running ——
Tenors   Running ——
Altos   Running ——
Perks   Running ——
All on time!
All on time!

No. 9: All On Time Play-Off

The Lights cross-fade as the Cottage comes into view

Perks exits

SCENE 6

Inside the Cottage

Mother is cooking something

The Children burst in, boisterously, still singing

Railway Children   All on time,
                        All on time,
                        All on time.

Mother What's going on?
Peter We went to the station!
Phyllis We saw a dragon! We saw a dragon!
Mother You saw a dragon?
Bobbie The train, Mother. Mr Perks says it's like a great green dragon.
Phyllis You said it first, Bobbie.
Mother Dinner is nearly ready, children. I have cooked for the first time in
my life, so the Lord alone knows what it will taste like. Now, Peter and
Phyl, you two set the table and I'll put some food out. Bobbie, maybe you
could help me? And Peter, could you get some more coal for the fire?
Peter If Phyl sets the table.

Phyllis tuts

Mother All right, you set the table. Bobbie, can you help me? Bobbie, I feel
a bit strange. Bobbie. (*She faints*)
Bobbie Mother! Mother! Peter, Phyl, help me. Peter, go and fetch the
doctor.

The Lights cross-fade

Perks appears

No. 10: You Might Make a Friend (1)

Perks (*singing*)   You're not quite in control
                            Of the journey you take
                            And at once you feel,
                            How the train starts to brake,
                            Then the speed that you travel
                            Has started to drop.
                            You have come to a halt
                            At a non-station stop.

The Lights cross-fade

Perks exits

Mother is in bed. Dr Forrest and Bobbie are nearby. Peter and Phyllis are downstairs

Dr Forrest (*to Mother*) It's nothing but the 'flu. It'll clear up in a week or two, but you'll need some looking after 'til then. (*To Bobbie*) Now, I suppose you'll want to be Head Nurse.
Bobbie Of course.

Bobbie leads Dr Forrest towards the front door

Dr Forrest Well, then, I'll send down to the village for some medicine. Keep her warm. Have some strong beef tea made up ready for her as soon as the fever goes down. She needs grapes, soda water and milk, and you'd better get a bottle of the best brandy. Cheap brandy is worse than poison, and I should know. There's a few other things she'll need to get better. I've written them out for you here. I'll come back in a few days and see how she is and you're to come and get me if anything changes. Understand?
Bobbie Yes, Doctor. Thank you, Doctor.
Phyllis You're a darling.
Dr Forrest Now, goodbye.

Dr Forrest exits

Bobbie goes to Mother

Bobbie The doctor says that you're to have the things on this list.

Mother reads the list

Mother Nonsense. I can't afford all this. Tell Mrs Viney to boil two pounds of scrag end for your dinners tomorrow and I can have some of the broth. Here's a shilling for the mutton.

Bobbie moves away from Mother

Bobbie (*to Peter and Phyllis*) Doctor told me to get these things for her, but she says we can't afford it.
Peter Why are we poor? We never used to be.
Bobbie Mother says it's only for a little while. Something's got to be done, she needs this medicine. There's only us to help her.
Peter We can do without mutton. Robinson Crusoe didn't have mutton on his desert island.

Bobbie But even if we didn't eat at all we'd never get all these other things with our money.

Peter We have to think hard.

Bobbie We must be able to do something.

Phyllis I'm thinking really hard.

Bobbie I've got it! The Old Gentleman! We've waved to him every morning and he always waves back.

Peter We could ask him for help.

Bobbie But we'll have to attract his attention as he passes.

Peter So he knows to look out for us at the station.

The Lights cross-fade as the scene changes to the hill

No 11: You Might Make a Friend (2)

During the following Peter and Phyllis stand on the hill holding up a banner made of a sheet on which reads "LOOK OUT AT THE STATION". Bobbie moves C. Peter and Phyllis join Bobbie C. She reads the letter they have written

Perks (*singing*)   When you've no locomotion
And you've run out of steam,
And all thoughts of proceeding
Are a far distant dream.
With the fuel and the skills
Of a keen engineer,
You'll be back on your way
With a wave and a cheer.

Perks exits

Bobbie (*reading, speaking*) Dear Mr We-do-not-know-your-name.
      Mother is ill and she needs to get better,
      Doctor says she must have the things in this letter.
      We know no-one here and Father's away,
      But somehow we'll find a way we can pay.
      Mother won't tell us our father's address,

Peter   Frankly, dear sir, it's a bit of a mess.

Bobbie   If Daddy can't pay you, because we're hard up,
      Then Peter will pay you, when he grows up.
      Signed Roberta,

Phyllis   Phyllis

Peter   And Peter.

Bobbie PS Will you give the parcel to Mr Perks the Porter and say it is for the Three Chimneys and he'll understand.

The music fades. The Lights cross-fade to the the cottage

Perks knocks at the door. Bobbie opens it and Perks is there, with a large hamper and a piece of sweetbriar

Perks Delivery for you. From an old gent, down at the station.

Peter (*playing the young gent a little too much*) Thank you very much. I'm most awfully sorry I haven't got twopence to give you like Father does.

Perks (*taking the mickey*) I do say, that's perfectly all right. Absobloomin-lutely. I weren't asking for no tuppences meself! Just drop it. I'm sorry that your mum's not well, so I bought her this bit of sweetbriar. Tuppence indeed.

Peter Thank you very much. And beg pardon about the tuppence.

Perks Consider your pardon begged. See you all. Full Steam Ahead!

Perks exits

The Children rip open the parcel

Phyllis Wow!

The Children pull out items from the hamper

Bobbie Here's the beef tea!

Peter And the soda water!

Bobbie And the milk!

Peter And the brandy!

Bobbie And two chickens. We didn't ask for those.

Peter And some wine!

Bobbie And some roses! What a dear old gentleman! Look, here's a note.

No. 12: The Old Gentleman's Letter

The Old Gentleman appears at the side of the stage. He reads his letter

The music swells

Old Gentleman (*reading*) Dear Roberta, Phyllis and Peter. Here are the things you asked for. Your mother will want to know where they came from. Tell her they were sent by a friend who heard she was ill. When she is well again you must tell her all about it. And if she says you ought not to have asked for these things, tell her that I say you were quite right, and that I hope she will forgive me for taking the liberty of allowing myself a very great pleasure.

The Old Gentleman exits

The Lights come up on the hillside

Peter and Phyllis appear on the hillside with another banner, this time saying "SHE IS NEARLY WELL, THANK YOU"

The Lights cross-fade to the Cottage

Mother How could you? From a stranger.
Bobbie He's not a stranger, he's our Old Gentleman.
Mother But begging like that.
Bobbie We didn't beg, it was a very polite letter.
Peter We were using our initiation.
Bobbie We had to help you somehow.
Mother Now listen, we may be poor, but we have enough to live on. You mustn't go telling everyone about our affairs, it's not right. And you must never, never ask strangers to give you things. Now I shall write this dear Old Gentleman a letter to thank him, and you must take it to the Station to deliver it.

The Lights cross-fade as the scene changes to the station

The Mother and Children exit

Perks enters

No 13: You Might Make a Friend (3)

Perks (*singing*)   With each stop that you make.
                             Fellow passengers leave.
                             Are you sorry they've gone,
                             Are you quietly relieved?
                             But the spaces they leave
                             Will soon fill once again,
                             And you just never know
                             But you might make a friend.

SCENE 7

The Station Platform

Perks moves to the next scene

The Children enter

Children Mr Perks! Mr Perks!
Perks Hallo, there.
Bobbie Hallo, Mr Perks. We've come to give someone a letter.
Perks A letter, eh? Thought you didn't know anyone.

*Perks's children (Colin, Elsie, Ginger and Patch) and some other village
children enter noisily*

What are you lot doing here? You're supposed to be at home with your
mum.
Patch She said she couldn't bear us any longer, and we was to come down
here and get under your feet instead.
Perks Oh Lord. Here's someone else you don't know — these are my
nippers, and one or two of their friends. This here's Colin.
Bobbie Hallo.
Peter How do you do.
Ginger How do you do what?
Perks Ginger, I've told you before. Remember your manners. Introduce
yourself.

Perks exits

Ginger Hallo. I'm Luke, but everyone calls me Ginger well, because me...
(*He points to his head*) This here's Elsie, she's me older sister.
Children Hallo —
Colin And this here's Patch. Her real name's Gilly No-one knows why we
call her Patch. We just do.
Peter Patch? That sounds like the name for a dog.
Ginger Well, it's her name so that's all there is to it.
Elsie Why have you come to live at the Three Chimneys?
Bobbie Because our father's away on business and so we couldn't stay at
home.
Elsie Why not?
Peter It's for the Government.

Perks's Children Oooh!
Colin Is he a spy or something?
Ginger Bet he's a spy.
Peter We can't tell you. It's a secret.
Colin I bet we can get you to tell us.
Peter I bet you can't.
Colin I bet we can.

The Perks's Children tackle Peter to the ground. Colin sits on him

Perks's Children (*shouting*) Tell us! Tell us! Tell us!
Bobbie Stop it! Get off him! Get off him! Don't be beastly!
Phyllis Get off him!
Colin All right, all right! We believe you. You don't know anything.
Ginger What's "beastly" when it's at home?
Bobbie Beastly? Well, it's beastly. Perfectly horrid.
Patch (*mimicking*) "Perfectly horrid."
Elsie You lot talk funny.
Peter We jolly well do not.
Elsie Yes, you "jolly well" do.
Bobbie You talk funny. We talk perfectly ordinarily.

No. 14: Posh Talk

Colin (*mimicking*) "Perfectly ordinarily". You talk posh. That's what it is.
Perks's Children Posh talk.
Ginger And you walk posh
Elsie And you dress posh.
Perks's Children (*singing*)   Look at you
                     With your fancy talk,
                     And your fancy airs,
                     And your fancy graces!

                     Think you're grand
                     With your fancy walks,
                     And your fancy clothes,
                     And your fancy faces.

                     Look at you
                     With your fancy ways,
                     With your fancy pants,
                     And your fancy braces.

                     Acting posh with your fancy chat
                     Of your fancy days in your fancy places!

(To Bobbie)   Plays the lady very lah-di-dah,
Mum's called "mama" and her dad "papa"!
Gents and ladies, very upper class,
Take your fancy talk. and stick it —
Where it hurts the most!

Look at you
In your fancy world,
With your fancy friends
And your fancy kisses,
Ain't you grand,
With your fancy shops
And your "morning, sir",
And your "morning, misses".

Ain't you posh with your fancy this,
Ain't you posh with your fancy that,
Ain't you posh with your fancy chat!
Lah-di-da-di-da-di-da-di-lah-di-da-di-da!
Posh talk!

Peter   Think you're big,
Think you're clever,
Think you're really tough!

Bobbie Peter!

Peter   I'm as big,
I'm as clever,
Just as bloomin' rough

Bobbie Peter!

Peter   Just because I'm talking different,
Don't make me a toff.
Elsie   But your chat is so much posher.
Peter   Doesn't mean I'm soft.
(Speaking) Oh, you bunch of rotters!

Railway Children   Don't think we have a fancy talk!
Any fancy airs, any fancy graces,
We're not grand,
Don't do fancy walks,
Don't have fancy clothes,
Or no fancy faces!

Peter	I don't have any fancy ways,
	Any fancy pants,
	Any fancy braces!

Railway Children	We don't have any fancy chat
	Of our fancy days in our fancy places.

	We've seen ladies very lah-di-dah,
	We're not like them, don't you think we are,
Perks's Children	Gents and ladies very upper class,
	Take your fancy talk—
	And stick it —
Phyllis	Yes, we've got the point!

All the children act out being upper class. They repeat the "La-di-dahs" in various parts through the dance, and by all taking the mickey out of the upper classes, they make friends

All	Ain't you posh with your fancy this,
	Ain't you posh with your fancy that,
	Ain't you posh with your fancy chat!
	Lah-di-da-di-da-di-da-di-lah-di-da-di-da!
	Posh talk! Posh talk! Posh talk! Posh talk!

At the end of the number a few people arrive for the train that is due at the station

Perks enters

No. 15: Posh Talk Playoff

Perks Go on, get off my station, I've got trains coming in! (*Announcing*) Next Train is the 11.11 to Dover. The 11.11 to Dover due now. (*To the children*) Here she comes.
Phyllis What's this one called?
Perks This one. The snail. Takes commuters to London and back.

A Man enters, rushing

Man Does this train stop at Dover?
Perks There's going to be a bloody great splash if it doesn't!

The train pulls up, some people get on and off. The Russian, Szczepansky, and Mrs Ransome are amongst those who get off. Szczepansky walks along the platform and falls down. A crowd gathers, some of whom got off the train, and some of whom are just arriving at the station

Mrs Ransome Are you all right?
Szczepansky (*in Russian*) Can somebody help me? Please I am lost.
  (*Phonetic pronounciation: — Kto'-to pomo'zhei mnye. Pozha'lusta ya
  zabloodi'lsya*)
Gert What's he say?
Mrs Ransome Beats me.
Perks All right, move along. I'll attend to this, if you please.

Nobody moves

Szczepansky (*in Russian*) I am looking for my wife and child. (*Phonetic
  pronounciation:— Ee'schoo zhenoo' ee rebyo'nkoo*)

Gert What's he say?
Bobbie (*to Phyllis, a little away from the main action*) Phyllis, go and get
  Mother.
Phyllis But ...
Bobbie Go!

Phyllis exits

Perks It sounds like French to me.
Gert (*flirting*) And me, Mr Perks, and me.
Peter It's not French.
Perks When I went to Boulogne, they spoke like that. When I asked the way
  all they said was "*Parlez-vous francais?*"
Szczepansky (*responding to Perks' French*) Je parle français, monsieur.

The crowd fall silent in surprise

Perks Bloomin' Nora! Anyone here speak French? You, Doctor?
Dr Forrest Latin and Greek, that's me.
Perks Who speaks French?

*There is general chatter, then Bobbie steps forward, unsure of herself, but
realizing she is clearly the only person who can help. The crowd are
surprised that this girl might be able to help*

Perks Go on then, miss.
Bobbie J'm'appelle Bobbie.

During the following, Bobbie and the Russian keep talking in dumbshow

Gert What she say?
Mr Barrie Beats me.

Mrs Ransome What she say?
Szczepansky ... *un petit peu* ...
Mrs Perks What's a petty purr?
Perks It's a pet what purrs.
Mr Barrie Must be a cat.
Mrs Ransome Just fancy!
Mrs Perks He's got a cat? Is he a vet?
Bobbie ... *habite avec ma mére, ma soeur Phyllis et mon frére Peter* ... (*She indicates Peter*)
Peter *Bonjour, Monsieur.*
Perks It's a marvel what they teach 'em in London schools. All kinds of language.

Mother and Phyllis enter

Mother Bobbie, what's the matter?
Bobbie I'm not sure. I think he's Russian. He speaks French, but something else too. (*To the Russian*) *Ma mére.*
Szczepansky *Madame.*
Mother *Comment allez-vous?*
Dr Forrest Is he really a Prussian vet?
Bobbie No, he's Russian, Doctor.
Mrs Ransome (*to Gert*) Hear that? He's a Russian doctor!
Perks (*admiring*) She's quite authoritative, that young girl.
Gert So are you, Mr Perks. So are you!
Mrs Ransome Shush, Gert, he's a married man.
Gert Just because he's got food in the larder, doesn't mean he can't read a menu.
Mrs Ransome Gert!
Mother (*to Perks*) He's a Russian. He's lost his ticket. I'm afraid he's very ill. I'll take him home with me. He's really quite worn out.
Perks I hope you won't find that you're taking in a frozen viper.
Mother Oh, no. I know who he is. He's a great man. He's written books, many beautiful books. (*To Bobbie*) You run home and light a fire in the sitting room. (*In French*) *Venez chez moi s'il vous plaît.*

Mother and Szczepansky exit with the children

Gert She's a funny one that woman.
Mrs Ransome The things I see down at the Post Office. The places she sends letters to. There's something funny going on with her.
Gert I see.
Mrs Ransome And taking a man into her house like that and her husband away. It's shocking.

Gert Lucky thing!
Mrs Ransome And him a foreigner too.

Gossiping, they all exit

SCENE 8

The Cottage Garden and Kitchen

No. 16: Lullaby

Szczepansky sings looking at a picture of his wife. He sits a little way away
from the family, in a garden chair, whilst the family are inside

Szczepansky *(phonetic)*Teeshe, mily, nye plachi,
                    Ty tsyel ee nyevryedoomy,
                    Pyesnyoo kalybyel' nooyoo, slooshai,
                    Ty v rookah mamy.
                    Dolgo, daleko my brodeem,
                    At vozlyooblyenny fermy,
                    Slooshai melodiyoo dooshi,
                    Ty v rookah mamy.

The 'l' is a soft consonant, pronounced as you would have to in the
collocation 'lyet'.

(Transliteration:)   Quiet, darling, don't cry,
                         You're safe and sound,
                         Listen to the lullaby,
                         You're in mummy's arms.
                         Long time, distant we have wandered,
                         From the beloved farm,
                         Listen to the tune of your heart
                         You're in mummy's arms.

Phyllis I don't want him staying in our house. Peter says he's an escaped
   murderist.
Peter I said he might be a murderist.
Mother He isn't a murderist — or a murderer —
Peter Well, what is he then?
Mother He's a writer. Of wonderful books. In Russia no-one dared say
   anything about things that ought to be done to make poor people happier.
   If you did you were sent to prison.

Peter But they can't. People only go to prison when they've done wrong.

Mother Mr Szczepansky, our Russian man, wrote a beautiful book about how to help poor people. I've read it. And they sent him to prison for it. He was there three years in a horrible damp dungeon, with hardly any light. In prison alone, for three years.

Bobbie Mother, you're crying.

Mother I'm sorry dear, I just can't bear to think of a man being locked up like that, all alone.

Peter It sounds like something out of a history book. It can't be true today.

Mother It is true. They sent him to the mines in Siberia, an icy wasteland, where he was chained to other convicts, and they walked for days and weeks. And wardens went behind them with whips — yes whips — to beat them if they got tired. Just for writing a good, noble book.

Bobbie How did he get away?

Mother When the war came, some of the prisoners were allowed to volunteer as soldiers. But he deserted at the first chance he got.

Peter That's cowardly, isn't it? Especially when there's war.

Mother Do you think he owed anything to a country that had done that to him? He didn't know what had become of his wife and child.

Bobbie Poor man.

Mother While he was in the mines some friends managed to get a message that his wife had escaped to England. So he has come here looking for them.

Peter Has he got their address?

Mother No. He was going to change trains at our station, and he'd lost his ticket and purse.

Peter Do you think he'll find them? His wife and child, not the other things.

Mother I hope so. I hope and pray that he will.

Peter When he does will he go back to Russia, where he belongs?

Mother Oh, no he couldn't go back.

Peter But he shouldn't stay in England.

Mother Peter. Doesn't it make you proud that someone who can't live in their own country, who has lost everything, can come here and build a new life. Doesn't it make you glad to live in a country that is safe for him and his family?

Bobbie You're very sorry for him, aren't you, Mummy?

Mother Yes. (*Pause*) Dears, when you say your prayers tonight, I think you might ask God to show his mercy upon all prisoners and captives.

Bobbie To show his mercy upon all prisoners and captives. Is that right, Mother?

Mother Upon all prisoners and captives. Now be good and welcome him into our home.

She exits into the garden

Peter We've got to be able to do something to help him.
Phyllis What can we do? We're only children.
Bobbie I've got an idea.

Bobbie moves to the side of the stage and we see her dictating a letter to the Old Gentleman, as she did before

SCENE 9

The Railway Carriage and The Hillside

The Old Gentleman enters and is seen reading a letter from Bobbie

No. 17: The Railway Children

Old Gentleman (*singing*)   Ev'ry single day I see them watching,
Ev'ry day they wave.
How can I ignore the children wishing,
Asking for my aid?

On a hill so green,
There you stand my railway children,
How you cheer an old man's journey.
Small against the sky,
Make a wish my railway children,
Waving in the blue,
Wishes do come true.

Bobbie (*reading*) To our dear Old Gentleman. Mother has taken in this Russian man. We found him on the station. His name is 'Shpansky'. She says he wrote a book and people locked him up. He is looking for his wife and child, who are in England somewhere. Is it possible you could find out where they are?

Old Gentleman (*speaking*) Now, this Russian chap
Is it *the* Szczepansky?
Wrote a book, then locked in prison
Now, he's turned up here.
(*Singing*)   Yes, my little friends,
I'll try to help you,
And help Szczepansky too.
Watching from afar
Knowing of your father,
Knowing who you are,
Knowing your darker sorrow.

Bobbie (*speaking*) Signed Peter, Roberta and Phyllis.

The Lights fade on Bobbie

Old Gentleman   On a hill so green,
                                     There you stand my railway children,
                                     How you cheer an old man's journey.
                                     Small against the sky,
                                     Make a wish my railway children,
                                     Waving in the blue,
                                     Watch me wave to you,
                                     Make a wish and wave,
                                     Wishes do come true.

The Lights fade on the Old Gentleman

   He exits

SCENE 10

The Cottage Garden

Mother carries a basket of washing out. The children enter from the house, with a picnic basket

Mother You don't mind going on a picnic, do you chickies? It's just that Mr Szczepansky needs some peace and quiet to get strong again.
Peter How long is he going to stay with us? He's been here a week already.
Mother He'll stay until he's better. Now you go off and have a lovely afternoon. I wish I could come. You know how your father and I love picnics.
Children 'Bye, Mother.

   They exit

Mother hangs the washing on a line. She picks up a man's shirt, her husband's, and holds it close to her, wishing she could be with him

   Bobbie enters, and watches Mother who begins to cry

Bobbie I forgot the cakes. Mother? Are you crying?
Mother No, dear. No, I'm not crying. I was just thinking of the picnics we used to go on together. The whole family.
Bobbie Mother. Daddy isn't — dead is he?
Mother No, my darling. Daddy was quite well when I last heard from him.

Bobbie Then why are you giving Mr Szczepansky his clothes?
Mother He hasn't got a thing to wear.
Bobbie But why didn't Daddy take his clothes?
Mother I asked you not to ask any questions, didn't I?
Bobbie Yes, Mother. Sorry. You miss Daddy, don't you?
Mother I miss him so much.
Bobbie (*to off*) You go on, I'll follow in a minute. (*To Mother*) I'll go and
get the cakes.

She exits into the house

Mother hangs the shirt, then another, but can't stop crying

Bobbie enters with the cakes

Mother, what's the matter?
Mother Bobbie, you and the others haven't forgotten Father, have you?
You never talk about him like you used to.
Bobbie Of course we haven't forgotten him. We did talk about him, but
whenever we did you seemed to get upset. So we stopped. We often talk
about him when we are on our own.
Mother Bobbie, you must never stop talking about him. You don't upset
me.
Bobbie You know we love him. And you.
Mother Bobbie, as well as Father being away something terrible has
happened.
Bobbie We're with you, Mother.
Mother Yes, you are. Peter and Phyl are too young to truly understand. But
you, Bobbie, you are different. Now off you go. Don't worry about me.
Bobbie But I do, Mother, I do worry about you.

No. 18: 'Til the Day

Mother kisses Bobbie on the forehead and sends her on her way

Bobbie exits

Mother (*singing*)   One look in your eyes,
                                One look at your smile,
                                One look at your face,
                                And I see him.

I know of a man like my father,
Met a girl and told her he'd always be there.
I know of the life that he promised,
Small suburban fantasies they both longed to
    share.
I know how she followed her mother,
Nurturing a daughter of her own.
I know all the dreams the young girl cherished,
How did that girl find herself alone?

I know there's a place that we've made here,
Somewhere we are living, somehow not a
    home.
I know every day that we spend here,
Leads me to tomorrow and to children who are
    grown.
I know, though we welcome the morning,
Evening is the harder time to bear.
I know in the darkness of the night time,
The only hope I have is that you care.

'Til the day that you come here,
'Til the day you return,
'Til the day this house echoes with your
    laughter,
'Til the day when you come home.

I know of the woman you married,
Thought herself a mother, thought herself a
    wife.
I know of the girl that you deserted,
Thought herself a future, and then thought
    herself a life.
I know there's a woman who waits here,
For the man who made her life complete,
I know that a woman on her own here
Has found herself a reason not to weep.

'Til the day that you come here,
'Til the day you return,
'Til the day this house echoes with your
    laughter,
'Til the day when you come home.

Mother exits

SCENE 11

The Hillside. Outside the Tunnel

The entrance to the tunnel is visible

The Children are having a picnic

No. 19: Act One Finale

Peter If it wasn't for the railway at the bottom it would be as if man had never been here.
Phyllis Except for us.
Bobbie It's beautiful here.
Peter Another sandwich, Bobbie?
Bobbie Thank you. Do you know that the Perks' children don't call them sandwiches, they call them "sarnies".
Phyllis Sarnies?
Peter What kind of a word is that?
Phyllis Another "sarnie" Bobbie?
Bobbie Thank you.
Peter And they say *we* talk funny!
Phyllis Do you think we'll see the Old Gent ——
Bobbie Stop. Shush! What's that?
Phyllis What?
Bobbie That noise?
Peter Look! That tree over there, it's walking!
Phyllis Don't be silly!
Peter Look it is!
Bobbie It's like the woods in *Macbeth*!
Phyllis I always knew the railway was enchanted.
Peter It's all coming down.
Phyllis It's too much magic for me.

The Children stand to see what is happening

Peter Isn't it exactly like when the coals come in?
Bobbie A landslide!

Part of the landslide is seen coming across the stage. It settles and stops

Look what a mound it has made.
Peter Right across the line!
Bobbie Yes. Yes. (*Pause*) The 11.29 hasn't gone by yet. The Old Gentleman's train! We must let them know at the station or there'll be an accident. Let's run.

Peter Come back! No time. It's nearly due. Couldn't we climb up a
telegraph pole and do something to the wires?
Bobbie We don't know how.
Peter They do it in war. I know I've read about it.
Bobbie They only cut them and that doesn't do any good.
Phyllis We could wave.
Bobbie They'll think it's us as usual. We've waved so often before.
Peter If only we had something red, we could wave it. Then they'd know.
But it would have to be something red.
Bobbie I know, our petticoats. Our flannel petticoats. They're red. Quick
Phyllis, take yours off.

*The Children come down on to the line. Bobbie and Phyllis take off their
petticoats. Peter takes Phyllis' petticoat. The sound of the train can be heard
in the distance, growing louder*

Phyllis Don't tear them.
Peter Shut up!
Bobbie Oh yes, tear them to little pieces. Don't you see, Phyl, if we can't stop
the train, there'll be an accident and people will be killed.

Bobbie and Peter tear each petticoat into three pieces

Now we've got six flags.
Peter We've got two minutes. These are my two.
Phyllis They're bigger than mine.
Bobbie It doesn't matter as long as we can stop the train. Here it comes.
Wave! Wave!

They wave the flags. Bobbie is on the line, Peter and Phyllis to the side

Peter Don't stand on the line.
Bobbie They won't see us. They're too high. They won't see us, it's no good.
Peter Get off the line, Bobbie!
Phyllis Get off the line.
Bobbie It's no good.
Phyllis Bobbie! Stop! Stop!
Peter Bobbie! Stand back! Bobbie!
Bobbie Stop! Stop! Stop!

*The train comes thundering out of the tunnel and comes to a halt, a few yards
from Bobbie*

Peter We did it.
Phyllis We did it. It stopped.
Bobbie Did it stop? Did it? I feel quite, I feel ...(*She faints*)

Bobbie faints. Peter and Phyllis rush towards her

The Engine Driver climbs down from the locomotive

The CURTAIN *falls*

ACT II
SCENE 1

The Station Platform

The Curtain rises. The Platform is decorated for a presentation. The entire village, including the Perks children and Szczepansky, are there. Perks is at a podium trying to bring proceedings to a start. Mother, the Railway Children and Engine Driver sit nearby. The Old Gentleman is in the village audience

No. 20: A Once In A Lifetime Day

Perks Ladies and gentlemen. (*He coughs*)
    (*Singing*)   Welcome ladies and gentlemen,
            We're here today to celebrate,
            The daring deeds of these brave children,
            And I would like to tell you straight —
            They saved the train from disaster,
            From crashing into earth and trees.
            As the station's stationmaster,
            It gives me joy to thank you three.

    (*Speaking*) Remember this is
    (*Singing*)   A once in a lifetime day,
            A day to remember forever,
            Your once in a lifetime day,
            A day you'll remember whenever
            You're feeling blue,
            Or down in the dumps,
            Dropped in the stew,
            Or riding the bumps,
            When you think your life is a flop,
            Think of the day when you were on top!
            Think of your once in a lifetime day!

Perks presents each of the railway children with a boxed watch and medal. The Villagers clap

    (*With a flourish*) And here is the Engine Driver to tell us exactly what happened!

Engine Driver Me? You want me to say something? Why didn't you warn
me?? (*To the Crowd*) Well, I haven't really prepared anything. You see,
I didn't know I was going to be asked! (*He glares at Perks but once he starts
singing he rather finds he is enjoying himself*)

(*Singing*)	I never saw it,
	Never heard it,
	Never saw a thing.
	Kept going faster,
	Into the tunnel,
	My smoky funnel was pulling us along t'ward
	disaster.
	I saw our three young friends,
	I didn't comprehend,
	'Cos they was all waving bloomers!
Crowd Bloomers?	
Engine Driver	Yes bloomers!
	And I thought
	"What can these bloomin' bloomers mean?"
	I pulled me brakes on,
	Pulled 'em right on,
	'Til the gauges turned,
	They turned to zeros,
	And when I looked up,
	Me train had stopped!
	And these three
	Were our heroes!
Perks	Our heroes!
Crowd	Our heroes!
Perks	A once in a lifetime day,
Engine Driver	A day to remember forever!
Perks	Your once in a lifetime day!
Perks	A day you'll remember whenever
Engine Driver	
Perks	You're feeling blue,
	Or down in the dumps,
Engine Driver	Dropped in the stew,
	Or riding the bumps,
Perks	When you think your life is a flop,
Engine Driver	Think of the day when you were on top!
Perks	Think of your once in a lifetime day!
Engine Driver	

Bobbie, Peter and Phyllis climb up on to the podium and address the crowd

Bobbie (*to Peter*) Remember. Just as we practised.

Peter	Ladies and gentlemen,
	We've something that we'd just like to say.
	It's awf'ly good of you,
Bobbie	We know we will remember today.
	And we shall treasure these watches,
	And these medals all our lives.
Phyllis	But we only did something so the passengers
	survived.
Railway Children	You have made today top-notch,
	So thank you, thank you for our watch!
Engine Driver	Our heroes!
Perks	Our heroes!

All (*excluding the Railway Children*) Our heroes!

(*Including the Railway Children*) A once in a lifetime day,
              A day to remember forever,
              Your once in a lifetime day,
              A day you'll remember whenever
              You're feeling blue,
              Or down in the dumps,
              Dropped in the stew,
              Or riding the bumps,
              When you think your life is a flop,
              Think of the day when you were on top!
              Think of your once in a lifetime day!

And in that way that can only happen in musical theatre, the whole village bursts into dance

              A once in a lifetime day,
              A day to remember forever,
              Your once in a lifetime day,
              A day you'll remember whenever
              You're feeling blue,
              Or down in the dumps,
              Dropped in the stew,
              Or riding the bumps,
              When you think your life is a flop,
              Think of the day when you were on top!
              Think of your ——

Sopranos ⎤	Once in a lifetime
Tenors ⎦	Once in a lifetime
Altos	Once, once in a lifetime,
	One lifetime
Basses	Once in a lifetime,
	One lifetime
All	Once in a lifetime day!

No. 21: A Once in a Lifetime Day Playoff

The crowd begins to drift away. There are different small groupings. The Old Gentleman talks to Mother, Perks talks to Bobbie and Phyllis

Mother (*to the Old Gentleman*) I want to thank you for that wonderful food you sent to us.
Old Gentleman And you are completely recovered now?
Mother Oh, yes. It was only 'flu.
Old Gentleman I understand how difficult things can be from time to time. In your situation. Is Mr Szczepansky still staying with you?
Mother Yes. He's here today.
Old Gentleman Would you translate?
Mother If I can.

Mother finds Szczepansky and brings him to the Old Gentleman

Old Gentleman Good-afternoon.
Mother *Bonjour, monsieur.*
Old Gentleman I have some news for you.
Mother *J'ai de bonne nouvelle pour vous.*
Old Gentleman I heard about your search for your wife and child.
Mother *J'ai entendu parler à votre recherche pour votre femme et votre enfant.* Children, come and listen.

The Railway Children come and join and other people drift over

Old Gentleman I have found them.
Mother *J'ai les retrouve.*
Old Gentleman They are living in Oxford.
Mother *Ils habitant en Oxford.*

Old Gentleman If you will come with me to London this afternoon —
Mother *Si vous m'accompagnez à Londres à l'apres midi —*
Old Gentleman I can take you to them.
Mother *Je vous emmenarai à votre famille.*
Szczepansky (*in English*) Thank you! Thank you!

He hugs and kisses the Old Gentleman, much to the Gent's surprise

Mother We must get you home and pack your things. (*To the Old Gentleman*)
Sir, we will meet you here in one hour.
Old Gentleman Very good.

Mother, Szczepansky and the others begin to exit, leaving just Bobbie and the Old Gentlemen

Szczepansky Thank you!
Mother *Monsieur.*

They exit

Bobbie Thank you. Why are you always able to help?
Old Gentleman I just do what I can.
Bobbie And no-one ever seems to reward you. They gave me this watch, but
who rewards you for helping Mother, or for finding the Russian's family?
Old Gentleman My reward is seeing a family happy.
Bobbie Mother isn't happy because Father's away. Mr Szczepansky and his
family are all going to be together and it makes me wonder when Father
will come home.

No. 22: (While You're) Busy Dreaming

Old Gentleman Your father will come home when the time is right. You
must be strong and patient for that day. And you must do whatever you can
to help him come home sooner.
Bobbie Why can't he be here now? Then we could live at home again. Like
before.

Old Gentleman   You can never go back to the past,
                           You must never repeat your mistakes,
                           You must always look to the future,
                           For the past has passed.
                           For while you're busy dreaming,
                           You think there's nothing for you to do,
                           Precious moments pass so quickly,
                           When your dreaming could come true.

For while you're busy dreaming,
Of the people you'd like to be,
There are others so busy,
Making their dreams reality.

Like a bird that refuses to fly.
Or a leaf that refuses to fall,
You can keep on planning forever,
But they're plans, that's all.

For while you're busy dreaming,
And making plans for another day,
Precious moments pass so quickly,
When your life can slip away.

For while you're busy dreaming,
Of the places you'd like to see,
There are others so busy,
Making their dreams reality.

Bobbie (*speaking*) But what can I do?

Old Gentleman   Be the one, be busy,
                      Making your dreams reality.

Bobbie and the Old Gentleman exit

The Lights cross-fade

SCENE 2

The Hillside. Outside the tunnel

No. 23: Paperchase Ballet

A ballet sequence illustrates the Grammar School boys' paperchase. One boy (the hare) dances first, then a group of boys (the hounds), followed by one straggling boy, Jim. The hare scatters paper to set a trail for the others to follow
Bobbie, Peter and Phyllis enter to watch them. Phyllis carries the picnic basket. They speak over the music

Phyllis I don't understand. If they're boys, why are they called hounds? Do they have dogs with them?
Peter No, silly. They pretend to be hounds and one boy pretends to be the hare, running away from the hounds.

Phyllis So why's it called a paperchase?
Bobbie Because the hare drops pieces of paper, like a hare drops a scent, so
  the hounds know which direction he's gone in.
Peter Look here they come now, you'll see.
Phyllis Why's it only Grammar School boys who do this?
Peter Because it is!
Phyllis Can we have lunch yet?

The Grammar School Boys dance into the tunnel

Peter Come on, if we're quick we can see them come out the other side.

*The Railway Children exit and the boys begin to dance out of the tunnel,
as if at the other end of it. The Railway Children enter to see the boys exiting
from the tunnel. One of the boys (Jim) does not appear. The rest of the boys
exit the stage*

Bobbie That one in the red jersey hasn't come out yet.
Phyllis Let's have lunch. I've got a pain in my tummy from being so hungry.
  You must have missed seeing him.
Peter Let's go down to the tunnel and see him.
Phyllis Can't we eat lunch first?
Peter We can't delay. If he's had an accident he might die.
Phyllis I'll die if we don't have lunch and then you'll be sorry.
Bobbie Here's a sandwich. That'll keep you going. (*She gives Phyllis a
  sandwich*)
Peter I'm sure he's had an accident. Perhaps even as we speak he's lying
  with his head on the metals, an unresisting prey to any passing express.
Bobbie Don't try and talk like a book.
Peter If a train comes keep close against the wall.
Phyllis Give me one more sandwich, then I will.
Peter I'm going first, it was my idea.

They enter the tunnel

SCENE 3

Inside the Tunnel

It is very dark and there are the sounds of dripping

Phyllis I want to go back. I don't like it here.
Peter There's nothing to worry about.
Phyllis It'll be pitch dark soon, then I won't be able to see anything. I won't
  go on in the dark. I don't care what you say, I won't.
Peter Don't be silly. I've got some matches and a candle.

Bobbie Maybe you should light it.

Peter lights a candle

Phyllis I'm frightened. Please let me go back.
Bobbie Would you rather wait here for us?

Phyllis shakes her head, a "No"

Peter Come on then.

They move further into the tunnel

The boy, Jim, comes into view; he is lying slouched against the wall

There!
Phyllis Is he all deaded?
Bobbie Killed? No. I think he's fainted. What are we going to do?
Peter Can we move him?
Bobbie I don't think so. He's a big chap. Suppose we bathe his forehead with water.
Phyllis We haven't got any water.
Peter We've got some milk. There's a whole bottle in the picnic.
Bobbie And they rub people's hands when they faint too.
Peter And they burn feathers, I know.
Bobbie What's the use of saying that when we haven't any feathers.
Peter As it happens, I've got a shuttlecock in my pocket. So there.
Bobbie Oh, look up! Speak to me, for my sake, speak to me!
Peter Wet his ears with milk. I know they do it with eau-de-cologne, but I expect milk's just as good.
Bobbie Oh, do look up.
Phyllis (*aping her big sister*) Do look up! I think he is deaded.
Bobbie No, he isn't. Come on, come out of it.
Jim (*waking and retching*) Chuck it!
Phyllis Oh, he's not dead! I knew he wasn't.
Jim What's all this? I'm all right.
Bobbie Drink this. It's some milk.
Peter Fear not! For you are in the hands of friends!
Bobbie (*admonishing*) Peter! (*To Jim*) Do drink it, it'll do you good.

Bobbie gives Jim the bottle of milk and he drinks some. He hands the bottle back to Bobbie who hands it to Peter

Jim I think I've broken my leg. One of those wires tripped me up. It hurts. How did you get here?

Bobbie We saw you all go into the tunnel and then we noticed you didn't come out the other side. We thought we should come and rescue you.
Peter It was my idea.
Bobbie Do you think you could walk if we helped you?
Jim I could try.

They try to help him up

Ow! Let me go! Let me go!

They put him down

It's no good.
Bobbie Look here! We must get help. You two go to the station. I'll stay with him. Give me the candle.
Peter I don't think Mother would like me leaving you. Let me stay.
Bobbie No. You and Phyl go.
Jim I feel strange. (*He faints*)
Bobbie He's fainted again.
Peter I hope it's all right, what we're doing.
Bobbie Of course it's all right, what else can we do? Leave him here alone? Now go. Hurry up!

Peter and Phyllis exit

Bobbie holds Jim

No. 24: Nothing To Fear

Bobbie (*singing*) Nothing to fear,
Nothing to fear, my friend.
Sleep in my arms,
Sleep in my arms, I'm with you.
I can calm the nightmare,
Tend your fevered brow,
Here in the dark,
Here in the dark, with you.
I can be strong, if I can hold you close,
Nothing to fear,
Nothing to fear, my friend.

The Music continues

Perks, Colin and other helpers enter lead by Peter. They put Jim on to a stretcher and carry him off stage. Peter follows

Bobbie remains on stage as the set changes around her from the tunnel to the Cottage

SCENE 4

The Cottage

Jim is discovered in bed, sleeping. Bobbie moves to the staircase where she meets Dr Forrest, coming from the bedroom

Dr Forrest Now, I sent Peter and Phyllis for some medicine for him. Your mother's gone to the station, to meet a relative of Jim's. His leg is fractured. I have set it but it will take a while to mend, but so long as you give him the medicine, it shouldn't be too bad. I have to go and see Miss Gert, so I'm leaving you in charge. Give him two teaspoonfuls of the medicine twice a day. I'll come back later.
Bobbie Thank you, doctor.
Dr Forrest You were a good nurse last time.

The Doctor exits

Bobbie moves into the bedroom and sings to Jim

Bobbie (*singing*)   Now you look so peaceful,
                            Quiet, but in pain.
                            Troubles are past,
                            Troubles are past, my friend.
                            You can be strong, if I can hold you close,
                            Nothing to fear,
                            Nothing to fear, my friend.

Peter and Phyllis enter through the cottage door and move to the staircase, carrying a bottle of medicine wrapped in newspaper

Bobbie moves on to the staircase to meet them

Peter Here you are.
Phyllis We got it as quickly as we could.
Bobbie Thank you.

She takes the bottle and unwraps the newspaper. She notices a story in the paper. A sudden change comes over her

(*Quickly instructing Peter and Phyllis*) Go. Leave me alone. Go now. Quickly!
Peter Bobbie?
Bobbie Go!

Peter and Phyllis move to the kitchen

(*Reading the newspaper*) End of trial. Verdict. Sentence: "Seven years penal servitude". Oh, Daddy! It's not true! I don't believe it. You never did it. Never. Never! (*She falls on the bed crying*)

The Lights cross-fade to the kitchen

Peter and Phyllis sit talking

Phyllis I've never seen her like that.
Peter Girls are funny sometimes. It's probably having a boy in the house.
Phyllis But you're a boy.
Peter But I don't really count.

Mother enters

Mother Children. Ah! There you are. Good. Where's Bobbie?
Peter She's with Jim.
Mother I want her here as well. (*Calling*) Bobbie!

Bobbie enters. She looks as if she has been crying

Bobbie. My darling whatever is the matter?
Bobbie Nothing, Mother. Please.
Mother I've been to the station to meet Jim's grandfather. He's waiting outside. I'll bring him in. (*She opens the door*)

The Old Gentleman enters

This way please.
Phyllis Our own dear Old Gentleman! (*She rushes to him and hugs him*)
Old Gentleman Well, hallo there! Hallo, Peter.
Peter Hallo!

They shake hands

Old Gentleman Hallo, Roberta.
Bobbie (*quietly*) Hallo.
Phyllis I'm so glad it's you. When you think of all the old gentlemen there must be in the world, I'm so glad it's you. You're a darling.
Peter You're not going to take Jim away though, are you?
Old Gentleman No, not at the present. Your mother wants to nurse him herself.

Peter But what about her writing? There won't be anything to eat if Mother doesn't write.

Mother That's all right.

Old Gentleman We have made a little arrangement. Your Mother has agreed to give up writing for a little while and to become matron of my hospital.

Phyllis And leave the Three Chimneys?

Old Gentleman No. No, it is to be the Three Chimneys Hospital and unlucky Jim is the only patient. Naturally, I shall pay your Mother for running my hospital. Take care of her, my dears, she is one in a million.

Mother Peter, Phyl, why don't you take Jim's grandfather up to see him.

Peter Come on then.

The three of them exit

Mother Bobbie, what is it?

Bobbie runs to her and hugs her, bursting into tears

Bobbie? What's the matter?

Bobbie slowly produces the piece of newspaper from her apron pocket

Oh Bobbie, you don't believe it, do you? You don't believe Daddy did it?

Bobbie No.

Mother That's all right. It's not true. And they've shut him up in prison and he's done nothing wrong. He's good and noble and honourable and he belongs to us. We have to be proud of him and wait.

Bobbie Why didn't you tell me?

Mother Are you going to tell the others?

Bobbie No.

Mother Why?

Bobbie Because —— (*Pause*)

Mother Exactly. So you understand why I didn't tell you. We two must help each other to be brave.

Bobbie Yes. Will it make you more unhappy if you tell me all about it? I want to understand.

Mother You know Daddy worked for the Government.

Bobbie Yes

Mother Do you remember the night Daddy went away?

Bobbie Yes. It was Christmas.

Mother Those two men who came to see Daddy were policemen. They arrested him.

Bobbie Why?

Mother They accused him of being a spy and a traitor, of selling State secrets to the Russians. There was a trial and the policemen said there were letters found in Daddy's desk, letters that convinced the jury that Daddy was guilty.

Bobbie How could they look at him and believe it?

Mother Sometimes the most pleasant looking people can be the most deceptive. Someone did it and all the evidence was against Father. Those letters ——

Bobbie How did the letters get into his desk?

Mother Someone must have put them there. The person that put them there must be the one who is really guilty.

Bobbie Perhaps he just shoved the letters into the desk when he thought he was going to be found out. Why don't you tell the lawyers or someone that it must have been that man?

Mother No-one will listen. Nobody at all. Don't you think I've tried everything?

No. 25: One Voice (Part 1)

Bobbie Is there nothing we can do?

Mother All we can do is to wait for him to be free and remember the wonderful times we used to have together.

Bobbie (*singing*)   For while you're busy dreaming,
                          You think there's nothing for you to do,
                          Precious moments pass so quickly,
                          When your dreaming could come true.

(*Speaking*) Maybe it is time to stop waiting. Maybe our dear Old Gentleman can help. I know he'd want to. Please let me ask him.

Mother Bobbie, we can't ask any more of him. He's been so good to us already.

Bobbie (*singing*)   And while you're busy dreaming,
                          Of the person you'd like to see,
                          There are others so busy,
                          Making their dreams reality.

(*Speaking*) Please. I know he'll understand.

Mother If this is the last time you ever ask him for anything. Promise?

Bobbie Oh Mother, I promise.

Bobbie exits

Mother (*singing*)   'Til the day that you come here,
                           'Til the day you return,
                           'Til the day this house echoes with your
                              laughter,
                           'Til the day when you come home.

Mother exits

SCENE 5

The Cottage Garden

The Old Gentleman and Bobbie enter the garden already in conversation

Old Gentleman When I read of your Father's case in the papers, I had my
doubts.
Bobbie You knew?
Old Gentleman Ever since I've known who you are. I haven't done as much
as I would like, but I have hopes, my dear. I just hope they are not false
hopes.
Bobbie I know you can do something. You don't think Father did it, do you?
Please say you don't think he did.
Old Gentleman My dear, I'm perfectly certain he didn't. There is a poem,
that your friend Szczepansky wrote. You should know it
(*Speaking*)   One voice, when it echoes a heartbeat,
                          When it breaks a silence,
                          When it cuts through the night,
                          One voice, if you join with another,
                          If you sing together,
                          If you sing clear and bright ——
(*Singing*)   Singing through the darkness,
                          Singing out for justice,
                          Singing loud, a clear and honest song,
                          Can right a wrong.

The Old Gentleman and Bobbie exit.

Perks enters

Perks (*Singing*)   In the carriage you travel,
                          You're rarely alone
                          A stranger, at first,
                          Becomes someone you know.

You can never be sure
Of the friends that you'll make,
In the railway vans
Of the journeys you take.

Perks exits

*Bobbie, Mother, Peter, Phyllis and Jim enter. Jim's leg is in plaster. Bobbie
and Mother are carrying luggage for their trip to London*

Peter I don't understand why Bobbie gets to go to London with you and we
don't. I am old enough.
Bobbie You don't even know why we are going.
Peter I am old enough to know if Bobbie is.
Phyllis And me.
Peter No you are not.
Mother I have asked Bobbie to come with me. You will understand when
you are older. You have to stay here and look after Jim for me. You can do
that, can't you?
Phyllis I can! He's a darling.
Mother Come along, Bobbie.
Bobbie Just a moment.

Mother moves into darkness outside the cottage

(*Turning to Jim*) I hope they don't drive you crazy. I'll see you later tonight.
Jim (*to Bobbie*) You look after yourself. I'll miss you.
Peter ⎫
         ⎬ (*together*) Ooooo!
Phyllis ⎭

Jim, Peter and Phyllis exit

Bobbie moves to join Mother

The Lights cross-fade and the scene changes to the train

SCENE 6

The Train Carriage

No. 26: One Voice (Part 2)

Mother (*singing*)   One voice, when it echoes a heartbeat,
                          When it breaks a silence,
                          When it cuts through the night——
                          One voice,

Mother ⎤ **Bobbie** ⎦	If you join with another, If you sing together, If you sing clear and bright—— Singing through the darkness, Singing out for justice, Singing loud, a clear and honest song, Can right a wrong.

SCENE 7

A London Street

The Old Gentleman enters and meets Mother and Bobbie

Old Gentleman I have news. Whether or not it is good it is too early to tell. It seems that the clerk who worked under your husband seemed to bear a grudge against him. I'm not sure why, but these things sometimes happen.

Mother He did mention someone.

Old Gentleman He seems to have been jealous of your husband's recent promotion.

Mother And now this man has been promoted?

Old Gentleman He has, yes, but he has been rather foolish too. He was seen two days ago talking to a known Russian spy in the bar of a London hotel. I plan to go to the Home Office with my information.

Mother Will anyone listen?

Old Gentleman My dear, we will need to make people listen to us. We may need to petition the Government to make them review the case.

Mother How can I ever thank you for everything?

Old Gentleman My dear, Justice needs no thanks.

Mother Everyday more letters come, so many people supporting us. So many of them write to Bobbie.

Old Gentleman You have a remarkable daughter.

Mother steps forward

Bobbie and the Old Gentleman exit. Bobbie returns with a clipboard and begins unsuccessfully collecting petition signatures from passers by

Mother (*singing*)   Will you stand and watch injustice shattering
       conviction,
Passively stand by or turn away?
Will you watch your freedom slowly suffering
       restriction,
Aware of all the futures you betray?

Mother and Londoners exit

Bobbie moves into the next scene

She is met by Jim

SCENE 8

The Cottage Garden

It is evening. Bobbie sits with Jim

Bobbie We have nearly five thousand signatures on the petition. Your grandfather said we've done really well to get that many in a month, and is taking it to Downing Street next week.

Jim I wish I could have helped you. I feel so useless sitting here.

Bobbie I wish you could too. It would be more fun if you were with me. You haven't said anything to Peter and Phyl, about why Mother and I have been going to London so much, have you?

Jim No. Peter was pretty cross that I wouldn't tell him, but I told him if he was a real man he wouldn't ask so many questions. After that he was just quiet.

Bobbie Peter? How can anyone get Peter to be quiet? You must be special.

Jim Me? You're the one who's special. I've never met anyone like you.

Bobbie Jim. Don't.

Jim I am so proud of everything you are doing for your father.

No. 27: One Voice (Part 3)

Bobbie You know, the worst part is all the people who don't even think there should be an appeal. The ones that think he should be kept in jail forever.

SCENE 9

A London street

Mother enters. A mob is devouring the latest edition of the newspaper

Customer (*singing*)   What a tale, it's very clear
There's a juicy story here
A story quite so sordid
It could not go unrecorded

Lady   A dreadful tale
True! True!
Headline news
On sev'ral nights —
Russian spies.

Gossip	Russian spies, Who would believe — Despicable! Even more? Darkest night. Russian spies.
Housewife	Bless my eyes. What a tale, And there's more ... Darkest night. Russian spies.
Vendor	Read it here! Read it here! Darkest night.
Customer	It's a tale of Russian spies, Of mistrust and outright lies The story is a winner, The story of the vodka stinger, It may also come to light, That over sev'ral winter nights. He may have met a henchman, A Frenchman.
All	Clearly this is espionage!
Sopranos	He should face his Judgement Day. Make him face his Judgement Day. Punish ev'ry treason Lock him up.
Altos	Sing out, we should all sing for justice Sing out, we should all sing for justice Punish, lock him up.
Men	He should face his Judgement Day. Make him face his Judgement Day. Punish ev'ry treason. They should jail him with good reason.
All	Yes, it's clear, Give him life!

Unable to bear this hatred any more Mother rails at the mob

Mother   Can't you think of his children,
                            Innocent in their shame?
                            Think only of his children,
                            Will you punish them with his name.
                            Storm clouds clamouring,
                            Round a family home.
                            Darkness gathering,
                            Casting them alone.
                            Punish the little children,
                            Bay for their father's blood.
                            That's what a pack of wolves would do.
                            We were once all children too.

*There is an embarrassed silence, as the mob are shamed by their previous
sentiments. After a moment, Bobbie's voice cuts through the silence. Slowly
Londoners join with her until they all have come to rally to her cause*

   The Old Gentleman enters to join the cause

Bobbie   One voice, when it echoes a heartbeat,
                            When it breaks a silence,
                            When it cuts through the night,
                            One voice,
                            If you join with another,
                            If you sing together,
                            If you sing clear and bright,
                            Singing through the darkness,
                            Singing out for justice,
                            Singing loud, a clear and honest song,
                            Can right a wrong.

Lady (or Sopranos) One voice,
                            If you join with another,
                            If you sing together,
                            If you sing clear and bright,
                            Singing through the darkness,
                            Singing out for justice,
                            Singing loud, a clear and honest song,
                            Can right a wrong.

Gossip (or Alto 1) If you sing together,
                            If you sing clear and bright,

Through the darkness,
Sing for justice,
Singing loud, a clear and honest song,
Can right a wrong.

Housewife (or Alto 2) If you sing clear and bright,
Through the darkness,
Sing for justice,
Singing loud, a clear and honest song,
Can right a wrong.

Vendor (Tenor)   If you sing clear and bright,
Through the darkness,
Sing for justice,
Singing loud, a clear and honest song,
Can right a wrong.

Customer (Bass)   Through the darkness,
Sing for justice,
Singing loud, a clear and honest song,
Can right a wrong.

Bobbie   Will you stand and watch injustice shattering
                              conviction,
Passively stand by or turn away?
Will you watch your freedom slowly suffering
                              restriction,
Aware of all the futures you betray?
Will you fight to rid the world of sorrow?
Strive to build a new tomorrow,
Starting with a promise made today.

All   One voice, when it echoes a heartbeat,
When it breaks a silence,
When it cuts through the night,
One voice,
If you join with another,
If you sing together,
If you sing clear and bright,
Singing through the darkness,
Singing out for justice,
Singing loud, a clear and honest song,
Can right a wrong.

SCENE 10

No. 28: In the Garden

Jim and Peter enter carrying two suitcases, ready for Jim to return to school.
They laugh and joke. Bobbie and Phyllis enter a little later

Bobbie I can't believe you are leaving us already. Don't forget us.
Jim How could I?

Mother enters

Mother Now, do you have everything?
Jim Quite sure, thank you. How can I ever repay you for all your kindness?
Mother There is no need. It has been a pleasure.

Perks enters

Perks Are you ready? Don't want you missing your train.
Jim All set.
Mother Are you sure you don't want us to come down to the station with
   you?
Jim Yes. Thank you for everything. (*He kisses Mother's cheek; to Phyllis*)
   Goodbye, Phyl.
Phyllis You're a darling. (*She hugs Jim*)
Jim (*to Peter*) See you, sport.
Peter See you. (*They shake hands*)
Jim (*to Bobbie*) Goodbye, Bobbie. Thanks for all the chats. I'll miss you.
Bobbie I'll write.

Jim and Bobbie kiss on the cheek. Peter nudges Phyllis

Phyllis Now they'll have to get married.
Peter And have babies.

Perks picks up one case and Jim the other

Perks Full steam ahead!
Jim Goodbye!
Railway Children Goodbye!

They wave

Jim and Perks exit

Phyllis I wonder if the railway misses us. We hardly ever go to see it now.
Peter It seems ungrateful, we loved it before Jim came and we had someone new and exciting here.
Phyllis The thing I don't like is our having stopped waving to the Great Green Dragon and sending our love to Father by it.
Bobbie Let's begin again.
Mother We should get back to our lessons.
Bobbie Please, Mother, may we go and see the railway first.
Bobbie All right. Just this once. But come straight back.

The Lights cross-fade

Perks enters

No. 29: Who Knows What You'll Find

Perks (*singing*)   There's the sound of the whistle
                                          The train starts to slow
                                          Somewhere deep in your heart
                                          There's a truth that you know;
                                          That although you have left
                                          All your past far behind
                                          In the trip to your future
                                          Who knows what you'll find?

Perks exits

SCENE 11

The Hillside

The Railway Children start to run to the hill

Peter (*to Phyllis*) Hurry up, or we shall miss the train.
Phyllis I can't hurry more than I am doing. My bootlace has come undone again!
Peter When you're married your bootlace will come undone going up the church aisle, and the man that you're going to get married to will tumble over it and smash his nose in on the pavement and then you won't want to marry him.
Phyllis I shan't. I'd rather marry a man with a smashed in nose than not marry anybody.
Peter Look the signal's down. We must run.

The sound of the train is heard

No. 30: Underscore (The Great Green Dragon)

Bobbie Take our love to Father!

Peter
Phyllis } (*together*) Take our love to Father!

Bobbie Look there's our Old Gentleman waving.

Peter He's waving his newspaper.

Bobbie Well.

Peter Well.

Phyllis Well.

Peter Everyone's waving. Every single person on the train ——

Bobbie Is waving at us! Whatever can it mean? Perhaps the Old Gentleman told the people to look out for us, and wave. He knew we would like it.

Peter It's most extraordinary.

Bobbie Don't you think the Old Gentleman's waves seemed more significant than usual. Like he was trying to explain something by waving his newspaper.

Peter Explain what?

No. 31: Nearly Autumn

Bobbie I don't know. But I do feel awfully funny. I feel exactly as if something is going to happen.

Peter I know what's going to happen is that Phyllis's shoelace is going to come undone. Come on, we promised Mother that we'd come back for lessons.

Bobbie You go. I'm going for a walk.

Peter But Mother said. She'll be cross.

Bobbie I think she'll understand.

Phyllis You're going to get into trouble.

Bobbie Well, if I am, then I am. I don't think Mother will mind. I'll be back soon.

Peter and Phyllis go to exit

Peter (*half-whispering*) See, I told you she was acting funny about Jim. They're in love. That's how you behave when you're in love. I hope it never happens to me.

Peter and Phyllis exit

Bobbie (*singing*)   I've seen the leaves begin to fall,
                              And watched the clouds begin to form,

And swallows gathering at twilight.
I've felt the dew that's here each dawn,
And sudden rain that starts to pour,
The heat that's missing from the sunlight.
I've seen the harvest moon,
Smelled bonfires burning,
I can't believe it's nearly autumn
When it feels like spring!

I wish the buds would start to bloom,
I wish the skies would start to clear,
And quickly banish autumn showers,
I want the early cuckoo's call,
And caterpillars growing full,
And golden daffodils in flower.
My sentimental wish
Keeps on returning,
I can't believe it's nearly autumn
When it feels like spring!

Mrs Ransome enters on her bike

Mrs Ransome Miss Roberta, Miss Roberta, I was just coming to your house with a telegram. You'd better get down to the station and quick.
Bobbie The station? Why?
Mrs Ransome You'll all be going to the station when your mother gets this telegram.
Bobbie What does it say?
Mrs Ransome I can't tell you, Miss. It's addressed to your mother. I'm no village gossip. Honest. But you go to the station quickly, I'll take this to your mother and tell her you'll meet her there.

Bobbie (*singing*)   Is something wonderful in store,
                              Or is there magic in the air,
                              Or is that only a delusion?
                              Can the elation that I feel
                              Come from a young man's tender touch
                              Or is it merely an illusion?
                              And can a gentle kiss
                              Set my heart soaring?
                              I can't believe it's nearly autumn.
                              I can't believe it's nearly autumn.

SCENE 12

Station Platform

Bobbie arrives at the station

During the following the scene entire village enters in a state of excitement

The Doctor enters

Dr Forrest Good-morning, Miss Roberta, what a beautiful morning it is.
Bobbie Doctor, I've got this wonderful feeling something is going to happen.
Dr Forrest Well, maybe it is, lass. Maybe it is.

Perks enters

Perks Hallo! Miss Roberta, God bless you my dear! I saw it in the paper and I don't think I was ever so glad of anything in all my born days! One, I must have, Miss, and no offence, I know, on a day like this 'ere! (*He kisses her on both cheeks*)
Bobbie Mr Perks!
Perks You ain't offended, are you? I know I took a liberty. But on a day like this ——
Bobbie No, dear Mr Perks, I love you quite as much as if you were an uncle — but on a day like what?
Perks Like this 'ere. Didn't I tell you, I saw it in the paper!
Bobbie Saw what in the paper?
Perks I have to make my announcement, Miss. The train's almost here. (*Announcing*) Next train is the 11.11 to Hastings. The 11.11 to Hastings.

Bobbie (*singing*)   I can't believe it's nearly autumn

Mrs Perks and Perks' Children enter

Mrs Perks (*to Bobbie*) We're so happy for you, lovie.

The Old Gentleman enters from the Stationmaster's office

No. 32: Finale

All three verses join together

Bobbie   Is something wonderful in store,
                               Or is there magic in the air,
                               Or is that only a delusion?
                               Can the elation that I feel
                               Come from a young man's tender touch
                               Or is it merely an illusion?
                               And can a gentle kiss
                               Set my heart soaring?
                               I can't believe it's nearly autumn

Old Gentleman   On a hill so green,
                               There you stand my railway children,
                               Small against the sky,
                               Make a wish my railway children,
                               Wishes do come true.

Female Villagers   One voice, when it echoes a heartbeat,
                               When it breaks a silence,
                               When it cuts through the night ——-
+Male Villagers   One voice,
                               If you join with another,
                               If you sing together,
                               If you sing clear and bright—-
                               Singing through the darkness,
                               Singing out for justice,
                               Singing loud, a clear and honest song ——

There is much smoke and the sound of doors slamming

A few people get off. As the smoke clears Bobbie sees a figure. It is Father

Bobbie Daddy! Oh my Daddy!

Bobbie runs to him, they embrace. Then Father holds her away from him and looks at her, recognizing the woman she now is. They hug warmly

Mother, Peter and Phyllis arrive and join the general celebration

The entire company sing

Soprano
Altos   }

One voice, when it echoes a heartbeat,
When it breaks a silence,
When it cuts through the night,
One voice,
If you join with another,
If you sing together,
If you sing clear and bright,
Singing through the darkness,
Singing out for justice,
Singing loud, a clear and honest song,
Can right a wrong,

Tenor

One voice, when it echoes a heartbeat,
When it breaks a silence,
When it cuts through the night,
One voice,
If you join with another,
Sing together,
Sing clear and bright,
Singing through the darkness,
Singing out for justice,
Singing loud, a clear and honest song,
Can right a wrong,

Basses

One voice, singing
Breaks a silence
Cuts through the night
One voice
Join another,
Sing together,
Sing clear and bright,
Singing through the darkness
Singing out for justice,
Singing loud, a clear and honest song,
Can right a wrong.

Full Company

'Til you come home.

THE END

No. 33: Bows

No. 34: Encore. A Once in Lifetime Day

All

A once in a lifetime day,
A day to remember forever,
Your once in a lifetime day,
A day you'll remember whenever
You're feeling blue,
Or down in the dumps,
Dropped in the stew,
Or riding the bumps,
When you think your life is a flop,
Think of the day when you were on top!
Think of your ——

Sopranos }
Tenors }

Once in a lifetime
Once in a lifetime

Altos

Once, once in a lifetime
One lifetime

Bass

Once in a lifetime
One lifetime

All

Once in a lifetime Day!

No. 35: Playout

FURNITURE AND PROPERTY LIST
ACT I
Scene 1

On stage: Christmas tree
Drawing-room furniture
Exploding toy train set
Mince pies
Drinks

Personal: **Perks**: Station guard's whistle

Scene 2

On stage: Luggage. *In it*: a framed photo of Father

Scene 3

On stage: Cottage furniture including two tables. One set with food
Bed in bedroom
Stove
Oil lamp and matches

Personal: **Mother**: three apples

Scene 4

No further props required

Scene 5

No further props required

Scene 6

On stage: Pan of food on stove
Table settings

Off stage: Two banners made from sheets (see page 21 and 22 for details)
Large hamper containing beef tea, soda water, milk, brandy, two
chickens, wine, roses, note (**Perks**)
Piece of wrapped sweetbriar (**Perks**)
Identical letter (**Old Gentleman**)

Personal: **Dr Forrest**: doctor's bag , list of medicine etc.
               Bobbie: letter to **Old Gentleman**

SCENE 7

No further props required

SCENE 8

On stage: Garden chair
               Photo of **Szczepansky**'s wife

Personal: **Bobbie**: second letter to **Old Gentleman**

SCENE 9

No further props required

SCENE 10

On stage: Basket of washing including **Father**'s shirt
               Washing line

Off stage: Picnic basket containing picnic food (**Railway Children**)
               Cakes (**Bobbie**)

SCENE 11

No further props required

ACT II

SCENE 1

On stage: Podium
               Decorations for presentation
               Seats for **crowd**

Personal: **Perks**: watches and medals

SCENE 2

Off stage: Paper for paper trail (**Hare**)
               Picnic basket containing, sandwiches and bottle of milk (**Phyllis**)

SCENE 3

Off stage: Stretcher (**Perks, Colin et al**)

Personal: **Peter**: candle and matches

SCENE 4

Off stage: Medicine wrapped in newspaper
                 (Newspaper has story of Father on front page)

SCENE 5

Off stage: Luggage (**Bobbie** and **Phyllis**)

Personal: **Jim**: leg plaster cast

SCENE 6

No further props required

SCENE 7

Off stage: Clipboard (**Bobbie**)

SCENE 8

No further props required

SCENE 9

On stage: Latest edition of London newspapers for the **Mob**

SCENE 10

On stage: Suitcases (**Peter** and **Jim**)

SCENE 11

Off stage: Bicycle (**Mrs Ransome**)

SCENE 12

No further props required

LIGHTING PLOT

ACT I, SCENE 1

To open: Darkness

Cue 1   **Music No.1: Prologue** begins   Page 1
            Bring up spotlight on **Perks**
            Slow cross-fade throughout song to reveal house end of verse 2

ACT I, SCENE 2

To open: General exterior lighting

ACT I. SCENE 3

To open: Dimly lit cottage interior

Cue 2   **Mother** lights a lamp   Page 10
            Bring up covering spot on lamp

Cue 3   **Mother** sits and cries   Page 11
            Fade lights on mother

Cue 4   **Perks** "You'll return to the light."   Page 11
            Lights cross-fade to the next morning in the cottage

ACT I, SCENE 4

To open: General exterior

ACT I, SCENE 5

To open: General exterior station lighting

ACT I, SCENE 6

To open: General interior cottage lighting

Cue 5   **Bobbie**: "... fetch the doctor."   Page 18
            Cross-fade to special on **Perks**

ACT I, SCENE 7

To open: General exterior on station

ACT I, SCENE 8

To open: General exterior and interior on cottage garden and kitchen

ACT I, SCENE 9

To open: Exterior and interior on hillside and railway carriage

ACT I, SCENE 10

To open: Exterior on cottage garden

ACT I, SCENE 11

To open: General exterior on hillside

ACT II, SCENE 1

To open: General exterior on station platform

ACT II, SCENE 2

To open: General exterior lighting on hillside

ACT II, SCENE 3

To open: Dark inside tunnel

Cue 14:   **Peter** lights the candle   Page 45
             Covering spot on candle

ACT II, SCENE 4

To open: General interior in cottage bedroom

Cue 15:   **Bobbie** falls on the bed crying   Page 48
             Cross-fade lights to kitchen

ACT II, SCENE 5

To open: General exterior on cottage garden with darkness on area outside the cottage

ACT II, SCENE 6

To open: General interior in train carriage

ACT II, SCENE 7

To open: General exterior on a London Street

ACT II, SCENE 8

To open: Exterior on cottage garden; evening

ACT II, SCENE 9

To open: General exterior on a London Street

ACT II, SCENE 10

To open: Exterior on cottage garden

Cue 16:   **Bobbie**:"But come straight back."   Page 59
             Cross-fade to special on **Perks**

ACT II, SCENE 11

To open: Exterior on hillside

ACT II, SCENE 12

To open: Exterior on station platform

EFFECTS PLOT

ACT I

ACT II